A
VIDEO NOVEL
BY
RICHARD J. ANOBILE

PUBLISHED BY POCKET BOOKS NEW YORK

Book designed by Harry Chester Inc.
Frame blow-ups by Ryan Herz & Mark Henry

Another *Original* publication of POCKET BOOKS

POCKET BOOKS, a Simon & Schuster division of
GULF & WESTERN CORPORATION
1230 Avenue of the Americas, New York, N.Y. 10020

ISBN: 0-671-82754-5

First Pocket Books printing April, 1979

10 9 8 7 6 5 4 3 2

Trademarks registered in the United States and other
countries.

Printed in the U.S.A.

Henderson Production Company, Inc.

and

Miller-Milkis Productions, Inc.

Present

MORK & MINDY

Created by

Garry K. Marshall

Dale McRaven

and

Joe Glauberg

"MORK: HOUR SPECIAL"

written by Dale McRaven

Starring

Robin Williams

Pam Dawber

Conrad Janis

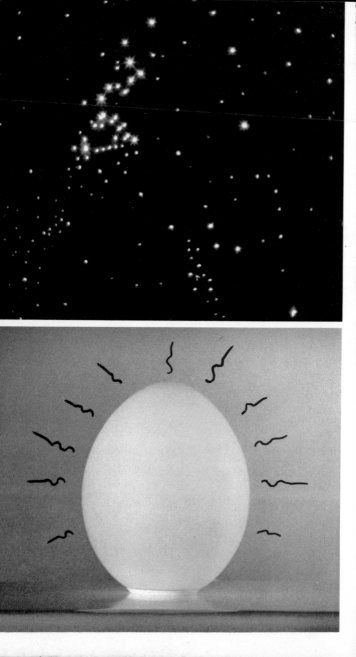

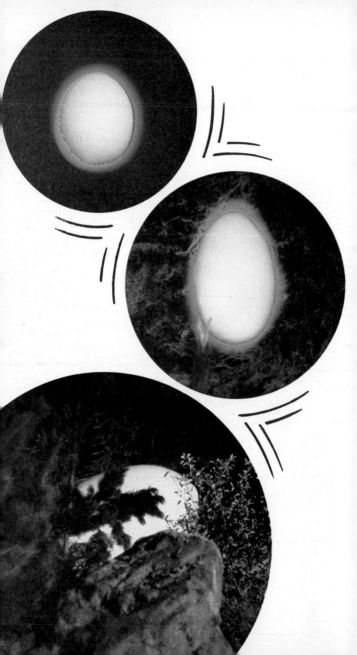

CRACK!

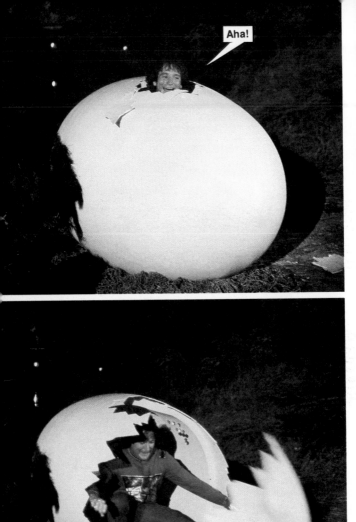

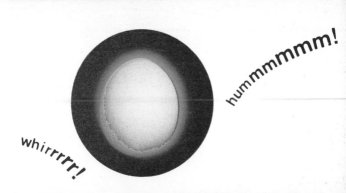

whirrrrr!

hummmmmm!

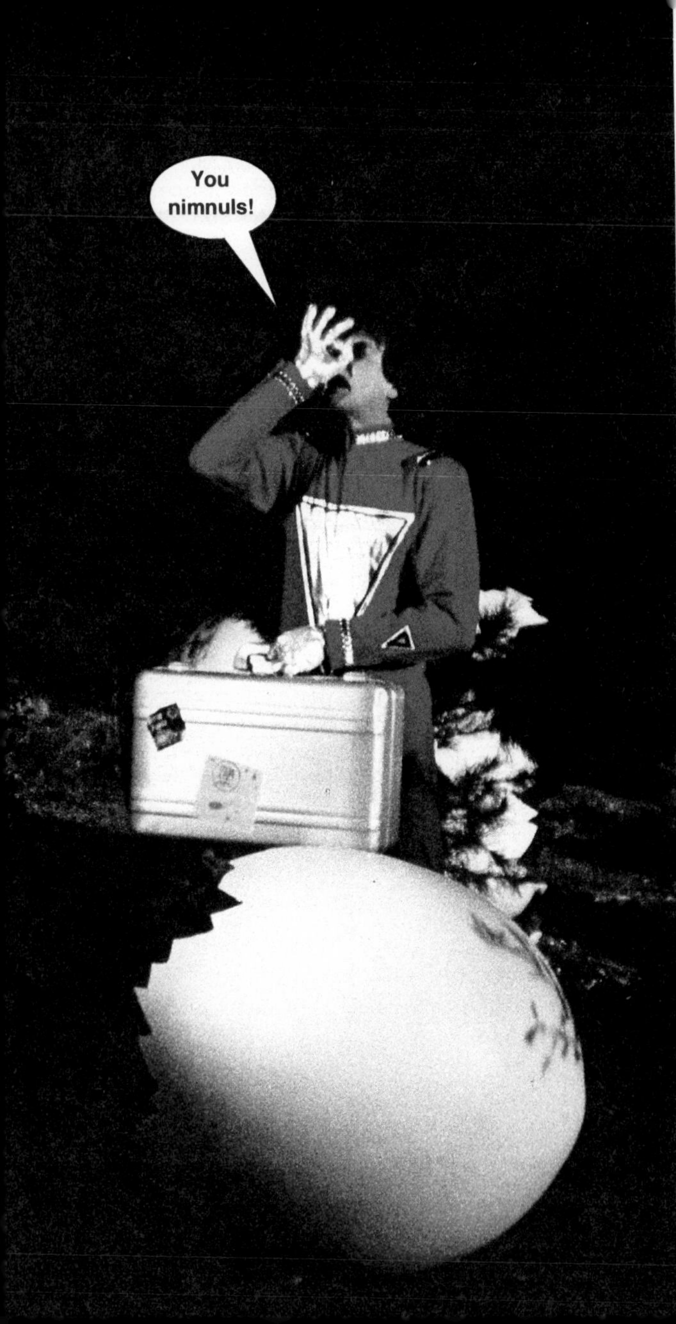
You nimnuls!

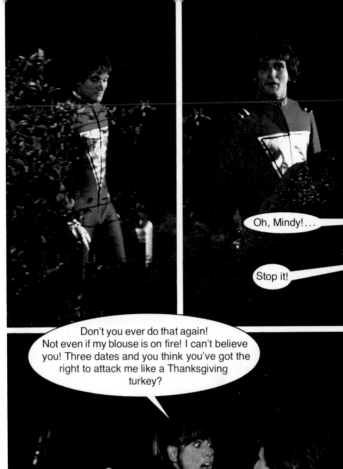

MINDY'S HOUSE

... LATER THAT NIGHT —

Well, here it is. Thanks a lot for walking me home, Father. I'm afraid I hardly gave you a chance to talk, but I was just so <u>mad</u>. You know what I mean?

Mad, mad, my pleasure. I was sent here to learn, you know.

Well if there's anything I can do for you …

Oh, if it's not too precious, a glass of water, and if it is, a quart of oil will suffice.

Oh … I think I can spring for the water …

Spring water! Humor!

Ark! Ark!

Up ... down ... hard to tell out in hyper space.

Oh ... right. I have a, a poor sense of direction myself. So, you ... you're from outer space!

How did you do that?

With my instamatic glove. Models starting under thirty thribets.

A fair exchange, let's formally close the deal.

SQUEAK!

... THE NEXT MORNING

Hello! Hello, anybody in there?

SPLAAT!

Well I had to. I didn't want to, but I had to do my duty. Do you think I enjoyed it?

This is about Mork, isn't it? What have you done?

Well, I, I just went up there to scare the little fellow. It's not my job, but when I seen him, I knew I had to do my duty. As much as I hated it.

Dr. Litney, if we may continue? What was your conclusion after examing the defendant?

Your Honor, my conclusions are ... that the patient is extremely childlike, ...

... and incapable of learning.

He has also exhibited marked anti-social behavior.

Ark!
Ark!

Then how do you know I'm doing it now?

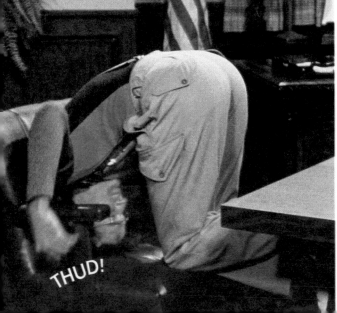

THUD!

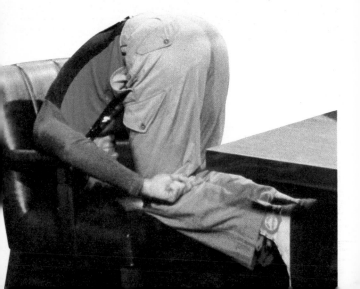

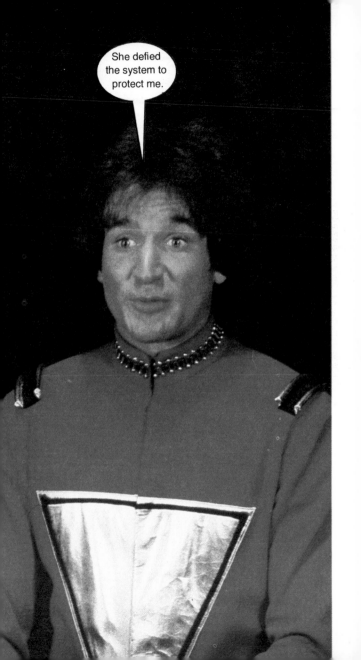

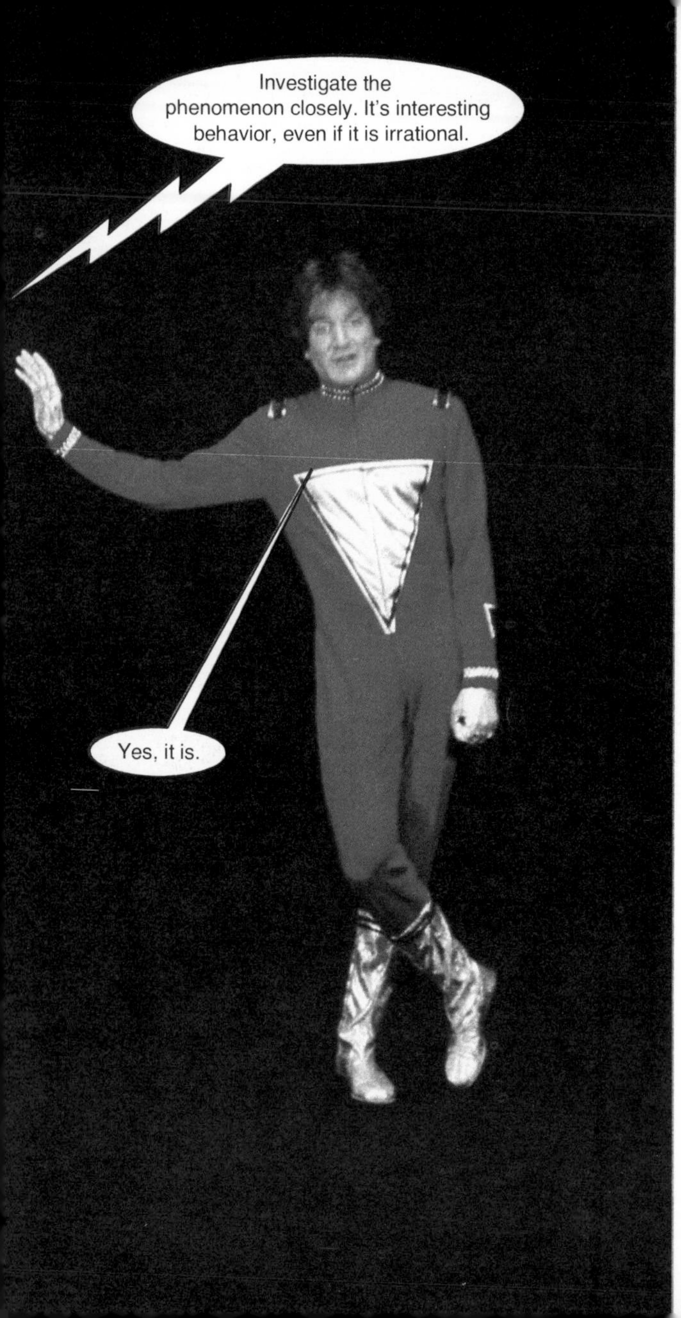
Investigate the phenomenon closely. It's interesting behavior, even if it is irrational.
Yes, it is.

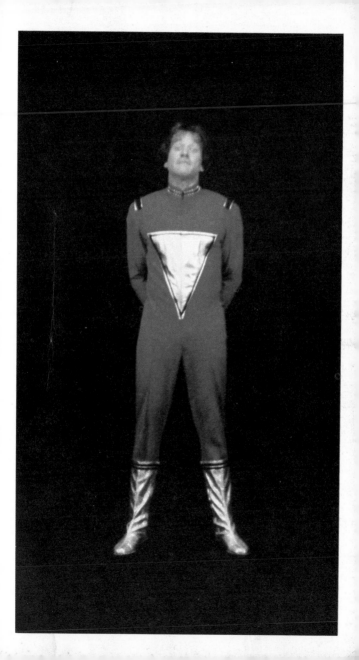